PROPHETIC MINISTRY BREAKTHROUGH

Student Workbook
Ministering Spiritual Gifts Series
Part 2

Available from:
Christian International Ministries
P.O. Box 9000
Santa Rosa Beach, FL 32459
1-800-388-5308
Printed in the USA

Table of Contents

INTRODUCTION

Student:
This workbook includes the following segments: prophetic principles, which are helpful in giving practical advice and answering common questions from the standpoint of the person prophesying; prophetic pitfalls which describes snares that can hinder ministers; and activations, which will give you the opportunity to minister spiritual gifts in a safe environment.

PROPHETIC PRINCIPLES

The Prophetic Principles segment will help you to be activated in prophetic ministry by breaking the power of fear; provide you with principles and practical advice for prophetic ministers and for those who are participating in and being exposed to prophetic ministry, and will expose you to proper principles for ministering personal prophecy.

BREAKING THE POWER OF FEAR

> *Jeremiah 1:7-8*
> *"Do not say, 'I am a youth,' for you shall go to all to whom I send you, and whatever I command you, you shall speak. Do not be afraid of their faces, for I am with you to deliver you, says the Lord"*

I. ACTIVATING PROPHETIC MINISTRY BY BREAKING THE POWER OF FEAR

____

____

____

____

II. FEAR IS ONE OF THE BIGGEST OBSTACLES TO EFFECTIVE PROPHETIC MINISTRY

Scriptural examples: Jeremiah 1:7, 8; Romans 14:23; Revelation 21:8; Proverbs 29:25

- Jeremiah 1:7-8: *"Do not say, 'I am a youth,' for you shall go to all to whom I send you, and whatever I command you, you shall speak. <u>Do not be afraid</u> of their faces, for I am with you to deliver you, says the Lord".*

  The phrase "<u>do not be afraid</u>," or some form of this phrase, reportedly occurs 365 times in Scripture.

- Romans 14:23, *". . . for whatever is not from faith is sin."*

- Revelation 21:8, *"But the **<u>cowardly</u> (fearful)**, unbelieving, abominable, murderers, sexually immoral, sorcerers, idolaters, and all liars shall have their part in the lake which burns with fire and brimstone, which is the second death."*

A. DEFINITION OF FEAR

Definition of the word *fear*. Fear in the Greek is "deos," meaning **<u>cowardice</u>, <u>timidity</u>, or <u>fright</u>**. It does not mean a natural fear, such as falling off a cliff, or touching a hot stove. This word does not mean fearless. Fear here is cowardice.

____

____

____

B. DEFINITION OF COWARDICE

1) Definition of the word cowardice: **When something threatens you, you won't act; failing to act in the face of fear**. The opposite of cowardice is bravery. Firemen are brave; they act in the face of fear.

2) It's not a matter of whether you respond **in** fear; the key is **what you do** in the face of fear. Do you act or not?

3) Why is it that cowards are included in the same list as liars, idolaters, sorcerers, sexually immoral, murderers, and the unbelieving in Revelation 21:8? Why is it so important?

C. FEAR OF MAN

1) Cowardice; snare: a noose, by implication a hook for the nose. The picture portrayed here is not the kind of snare that traps an animal.

   - Proverbs 29:25, *"The fear of man brings a snare, but whoever trusts in the Lord shall be safe."*

ILLUSTRATION:

Picture a big water buffalo and a little child leading it across the rice patty. Water buffalo are some of the most dangerous animals in the world. They are very aggressive and powerful by temperament. How is this child leading the water buffalo around? A hook is placed through the animal's nose, and then closed off, and a ring is made with a little rope tied to it. Just a little tug on the rope and the animal will follow you. It's the most sensitive place on the animal and it hurts so the animal won't buck against it. The hook in the nose completely controls this very powerful animal with this little puny kid leading it around because it made a snare. It found a sensitive point and hooked right in.

If we have wounds, an open place, or a weakness, the enemy loves to come in and take advantage of it and put a hook in it. So every time you try to pull away, you can't because it hurts. When you sin it causes shame in your life. Shame by definition brings fear. You try hard to cover your sin. So you are afraid, and instead of overcoming your fear, you try hard to control your environment. When you try to control people for selfish means, it is sin. It becomes an endless cycle of SHAME/FEAR/CONTROL.

SUMMARY:
Fear brings a snare. It controls you by keeping you from doing what you are supposed to do.

Fear is anti-faith. Faith is doing something. Faith without works is dead. Cowardice is not acting because you are afraid. Fear kills faith because you don't act.

____

____

____

____

____

III. THE SCRIPTURAL ANTIDOTE TO FEAR

Scriptural examples: 2 Timothy 1:6, 7; Romans 15:19; 1 John 4:18

- 2 Timothy 1:6-7:
  "Therefore I remind you to stir up the gift of God which is in you through the laying on of my hands. For God has not given us a spirit of fear, but of <u>power</u> and of <u>love</u> and of a sound <u>mind</u>."

When you try to stir up the gift of God, you will have to face fear. Some translations use the word timidity, which is a form of cowardice, so we know this is not a natural fear of harm. God has given us this **"antidote cocktail"** to help overcome fear: **power, love, and a sound mind**.

A. POWER: Greek word is dunamis, which means miraculous power.

Romans 15:19:
"in mighty signs and wonders, by the power of the Spirit of God, so that from Jerusalem and round about to Illyricum I have fully preached the gospel of Christ."

1) The distinction between preached and fully preached is that when you fully preach, you are preaching with mighty signs and wonders in the power of the Spirit.

2) ILLUSTRATION:

   You are by yourself in your home relaxing. Someone breaks in your home and they have a knife. This is a fear invoking situation. You happen to be loading your gun at that moment, your Smith and Wesson 357 Magnum, so it's clean and ready to go. This guy breaks in with a knife. Does this change your level of fear? Does it change his level of fear? What changed, because he's still breaking in with a knife? The difference is that you have ***power****. You change you are no longer experiencing fear in a way that makes it so that you can't act. In fact, you'll probably act immediately. If you know you have the power, then there's no reason not to act, and you'd be brave.*

3) In the same way, we have to be convinced in our hearts and spirits that we have the power within us. **Doing activations** is a safe place to test fire your weapon. When you fire it a few times and realize you are able to do it then you know you have power, which helps to overcome fear.

B. LOVE: Agape, means "**an unselfish commitment to the welfare of another, based on God's sense of value and worth for each person**."

1 John 4:18:
"There is no fear in love; but perfect love casts out fear, because fear involves torment. But he who fears has not been made perfect in love."

1) How does perfect love cast out fear? Look at the illustration again:

   You are in your house and the guy breaks in. This time he has the gun and you have no weapon. You are powerless. He's got the power. He's threatening you and you'll do anything he says. Right? You are going to try to survive and hope he doesn't hurt you. Let's change it a bit. Your child is in the room. Things change a little, don't they? You love your child, so now your whole goal is not saving yourself but your child. Before, if he had raised his weapon at you, you would have done anything to get out of the way of the bullet.

Now if he raises the weapon and points it at your child, you'll do anything you can to get in the way of the bullet. Perfect love casts out fear, because fear means not acting. When you love someone that much, you'll act even though you're afraid.

2) Additional verses on love: 1 John 4:20; 1 Corinthians 13

SUMMARY: Perfect love is about someone else. *Agape* means the welfare of another is your main commitment. When you get other focused, the gifts work by love.

APPLICATION: <u>When you prophesy you have to love the other person, even though you might miss it and look foolish</u>.

C. <u>SOUND MIND</u>: Sometimes translated as self-discipline, or mental discipline; Two Greek words which literally mean "**<u>to save the mind</u>**."

1) The **<u>mind</u>** is one of the biggest battlegrounds where spiritual warfare is waged.

Illustration:
Raising daughters is a fearful thing for fathers. You love them but they make you nervous in all kinds of ways, and one of those ways is when they are not around. Sometimes when they are not around, that's the worst. Because then you are sitting at home pleasantly waiting for that call that you instructed them to give at about 10 or 10:30, something like that, and it's about 11, and at this point you are just irritated. But at 11:30 you start thinking of ways to be afraid. Now you are pretty sure even this daughter would have thought to call. So now you start suspecting in your mind, maybe there's something wrong. Maybe they had an auto accident. Maybe the person she was out with is not really who we thought they were. Maybe she ran away or she's in the hospital or in a ditch on the side of the road. You start getting more and more afraid. Now they come in all happy and say oh, I forgot to call didn't I? And then you do act at that point. But there wasn't any real reason to be afraid except you started thinking things that made you afraid.

2) Being free from fear requires discipline and self-control of our thought processes. How does having a disciplined or self-controlled mind overcome fear? **Fear and faith are <u>opposites</u>. They are also similar in two ways: they are both about the future and they both begin in the mind.**

3) Scriptural Examples:

   - Romans 10:17, faith comes by hearing the word of God. "Word" here means the rhema word not logos. Logos means the written word, and rhema means the spoken word. Logos is scripture; rhema is the revelation that comes from God. Rhema can be a still small voice or a prophetic word from someone else. Faith comes from the rhema word of God.
   - Romans 12:2 says, do not be conformed by the world but be transformed by the renewing of the <u>mind</u>.
   - Isaiah 26:3 says, God will give you perfect peace when your mind is stayed on Him. Stayed means "steadfastly, devoted to."
   - 1 Corinthians 2:16 says that we have the <u>mind</u> of Christ.

4) Hearing God's word brings faith. Faith overcomes fear. Fear also begins in the mind. It starts with your thoughts - thoughts such as "what if?" "Did God really mean that?" "I thought" that's what the prophetic word meant, "I thought" I could minister that way. Every time we say, "I thought", it's not rhema. **When we dwell on what God says and let that become the focus of our minds, our mind is stayed on Him**. When we discipline ourselves and take every thought captive to the obedience (acting), that means we are not in fear.

➢ SUMMARY:

God has given us the antidote to overcome fear. You can use the ingredients one at a time or in any combination. All these things will help you overcome fear in your life and help you to act in fearful situations. You should not be condemned because you sensed fear. The first thing God said to Moses at the burning bush was "Do not be afraid." The first thing the angel said to Mary was "Do not be afraid." Our reaction to fear is what is important. Do you stop? Do you run away (physically, emotionally, and mentally)? Or do you act anyway? If you act, that's bravery, and faith.

IV. BREAK AGREEMENTS WITH SPIRITS OF FEAR

STUDENT: Your instructor will lead you in a prayer to break your agreement with the spirit(s) of fear such as: fear of man, fear of failure, fear of public humiliation, fear of exposure, fear of making a mistake, fear of being wrong, fear of retribution, etc.

- Ask the Lord to speak a rhema to you. Ask specifically, "What is it in my life that is making me not act in the face of fear?" Let Him address the main instigator of fear in your life. Write down what the Lord shows you:

  ____

  ____

  ____

  ____

- The process for freedom from demonic oppression is: Forgive others and yourself, renounce agreement with fear, and cast out these spirits.

PROPHETIC PROTOCOL

> *1 Corinthians 14:3*
> *"But he who prophesies speaks edification and exhortation and comfort to men".*

I. PROPHETIC PROTOCOL

A. DEFINITION OF PROTOCOL

Definition of the word protocol: Defined literally as "a code of diplomatic or military etiquette and precedence." When used in the medical field, it is defined as "the right way to do something." This does not mean it is the only way, or that there aren't other ways one could do it, but **in any setting, in any particular time or place, there's a good or right way**.

B. DEFINITION OF PROPHETIC PROTOCOL

Prophetic Protocol - defined as "**the proper administration and order of prophetic which, when observed, provides the person being ministered to maximum ability to receive and benefit from the word given**."

1) Notice that the focus is on the **receiver**. The whole reason for protocol is for the **receiver**.

____

____

____

____

2) Fed- Ex. Illustration:

As prophetic people, and those who exercise spiritual gifts, we are the delivery people. We are Fed-Ex. We don't make the prophetic words, God does. We don't consume the words, the receiver does. So as a prophetic minister, our job is to deliver it right. So using the Fed-ex analogy, the person who is delivering this thing from the manufacturer to the consumer, their whole job is to make sure the delivery goes well and gets where it is going in the right condition, i.e. not broken. You would be upset with Fed-Ex if they broke your package. What if they come at midnight, ring your doorbell, and say they have a package for you? You aren't very happy. What if they come to the wrong address at the right time or what if they bring it but don't put it in a box, it's kind of in pieces and you aren't even sure all the pieces are even there? So it's Fed-Ex's job to make sure it comes the way it's supposed to, when it's supposed to, and where it's supposed to, in the form it's supposed to. And after it's delivered, you don't expect the Fed-Ex people to come back and check on how you are enjoying the package.

C. GUIDELINES

____

____

____

____

D. NEED FOR PROTOCOL

Why the need for protocol?

Because prophetic ministry is a very <u>powerful tool</u>; prophetic ministry is like a laser beam, with the potential to <u>heal or destroy</u>.

1) Surgeons can take a laser beam and repair your vision. If done the right way, it makes your vision better. If done incorrectly, it can make you blind. The person performing the surgery has the responsibility to perform it correctly.

2) Protocol can be incredibly important because it **means you are <u>trying to</u> get the delivery made in a way the receiver can get it**. For example, if someone approaches you with a knife in their hand and a mask on their face, what do you think? Are you about to be mugged or about to get surgery? It depends on the motivation of the person and the setting you are in when this happened. It's all about the heart of the person coming to you and what you are hoping to receive.

3) One of the greatest dangers of the Prophetic Movement is **prophetic people ministering out of their own <u>hurts</u> or <u>wounds</u>**. (This is when the doctor described above turns into a mugger.) You are no longer motivated by the opportunity to heal, but by your own need for healing.

4) The right time, place, and way makes a difference as to whether your delivery, your meeting, or opportunity succeeds and that's what you care about, not how you appear.

5) Example of diplomatic corps. If you wanted to meet the Head of State, there are specific protocols for each situation.

    - The Queen of England: They would actually have a protocol officer there who would tell you what to do and they would tell you that when you meet the Queen, you don't speak first or initiate any physical contact. Don't put your hand out to be shaken; don't give her a big hug. Let her initiate everything. If you did the protocol right, you did well. If you changed your mind and didn't do it the right way, and you run off and give her a hug, there are men in fuzzy hats to help you understand the right way to do it.

- The King of Jordan: If you visit the King of Jordan, there is a different protocol. You would be told to step right up to him, put your hand on his shoulders, and kiss him on both cheeks. If you don't do that, it is likely to be insulting, because that's the traditional greeting and this is a formal situation.

II. WHEN MINISTERING IN PERSONAL PROPHECY, CARE AND WISDOM SHOULD BE EXERCISED WHEN REVEALING DETAILS OF A PERSON'S LIFE IN A PUBLIC SETTING

- When calling somebody out, we have a sacred trust to care for them and not embarrass or expose them.
- Prophetic people should never shame or humiliate individuals to whom they are called to minister.
- Some suggestions for those functioning in public prophetic ministry:
    - Use terms that allow the individual to understand clearly what God is saying, but which are not **critical**, **condemning**, **or** **exposing**.
    - Ask the Lord if you can take a negative and turn it into a positive, i.e. prophesy a person's potential instead of their history.

III. WHAT TO DO WITH CORRECTIVE AND/OR JUDGMENTAL WORDS

- Do not take the attitude that God has sheriffs in the body of Christ to make things right, and that you're one of those sheriffs.

- Understand that according to 1 Corinthians 14:3, prophecy is for **edification, exhortation, and comfort, not correction or judgment**.

- Understand the philosophy of ministry of your local church. Our philosophy at Christian International is that only those who stand in five-fold office ministry with maturity and wisdom will be used of the Lord to bring words of judgment and correction.

- Prophets who are eager to prophesy judgment are not candidates for this type of ministry.

- Note Samuel's attitude upon hearing from God that God had rejected Saul from being king. It grieved Samuel and he cried out to the Lord all night (1 Samuel 15:11).

____
____
____
____

IV. SPEAKING PROPHETICALLY TO THOSE IN AUTHORITY

Leadership protocol does come into play when ministering personal prophecy. While we should not over-emphasize "peer ministry" which limits who can share or prophesy, our experience has shown that several points should be observed in this regard:

1) The one ministering should be careful not to be presumptuous or have the wrong motive when ministering to those in leadership or positions of stature.

2) In a generation of abandoned people who have been hurt by authority figures, some may delight when leaders in the Body get their comeuppance (a deserved rebuke or penalty.)

3) Others have a "notch in the gun" syndrome which allows them to feel personally significant because they have ministered to somebody of significance.

4) Occasionally, prophecy to leaders needs to be given in a confidential context (and not in public), as the following examples illustrate:

    - 2 Kings 9:2-6 - The young prophet, at Elisha's instruction, anointed Jehu king in the inner chamber, not in front of the other captains.
    - 1 Kings 11:29 - Ahijah prophesied to Jeroboam that he would become the next king while they were "alone in the field."
    - 1 Samuel 15:13-31 - Samuel pronounced judgment to Saul in a private setting, hence Saul's request of Samuel to "turn again with me and worship" and to "honor me before the elders."

5) Did Samuel honor Saul publicly after judging him privately? Why?

____
____
____
____

- **PRACTICAL APPLICATION:** dealing with changes in leadership of local churches via prophetic ministry.

  It's a bad idea to do anything that might be interpreted as a change to that leader in public. Example: Pastor and worship leader - A prophetic word comes forth that God is going to take the pastor around the world apostolically and they are going to raise up the worship leader to be the pastor. The week after this word is given publicly the church is beginning to split. Pretty soon the sheep are scattering and wondering why the worship leader isn't the pastor yet. It could be ten years before this transition actually takes place. *You should tell the pastor later, in private.*

  Examples: 1 Kings 11:29; 1 Samuel 15

  ____

  ____

  ____

  ____

V. NATURAL AREAS OF PROTOCOL FOR PROPHETS AND PROPHETIC TEAMS

- Recognize and submit graciously to the pastor or designated team leader.
  - Show respect for fellow team members. Be attentive to their ministry. Don't stand in front of them, and don't contradict each other.
  - Learn how to handle the microphone by speaking clearly into it. Don't grab it out of someone else's hand, and don't interrupt someone who is speaking.
- Don't hog the show! Let others function as much as you do or more.
  - There is no letter "I" in the word "Team".
  - TEAM = Together Everyone Accomplishes More
- Try to be brief and concise. Don't go too long and preach a message or share your doctrine while prophesying.
- Lay hands on people with discretion and respect.
- When calling individuals out, be direct and clear to whom you are talking to avoid confusion. We like to have them stand, ask their name for the tape, then minister to them. Afterwards, say thank you and ask them to be seated. Do not identify them by gender, size, or race (physical attributes), such as "the big lady", "the bald guy", etc. The "lady in the back" may not be a woman! Instead, call out by position and clothing. For example: "The person in the 5th row on the end, wearing the plaid shirt."

ADDITIONAL NOTES:

Prophetic Pitfalls

God desires us to be faithful stewards and ministers of the gifts He has given to us. However, He is more interested in the character of the minister than in their ministry. With that in mind, the purpose of the Prophetic Pitfalls segment is to present teaching, using biblical examples of prophets and apostles, that will help the saints to 1) recognize root problems, character flaws and weed seed attitudes in their lives that could hinder their ministry; 2) recognize common deceitful and destructive pitfalls and snares that could destroy their lives and ministry.

CHARACTER FLAWS, WEED SEED ATTITUDES, AND ROOT PROBLEMS

Matthew 3:7-12

"But when he saw many of the Pharisees and Sadducees coming to his baptism, he said to them, "Brood of vipers! Who warned you to flee from the wrath to come? Therefore bear fruits worthy of repentance, and do not think to say to yourselves, 'We have Abraham as our father.' For I say to you that God is able to raise up children to Abraham from these stones. And even now the ax is laid to the root of the trees. Therefore every tree which does not bear good fruit is cut down and thrown into the fire. I indeed baptize you with water unto repentance, but He who is coming after me is mightier than I, whose sandals I am not worthy to carry. He will baptize you with the Holy Spirit and fire. His winnowing fan is in His hand, and He will thoroughly clean out His threshing floor, and gather His wheat into the barn; but He will burn up the chaff with unquenchable fire."

A. BAPTISM OF FIRE

We are living in a time when the Holy Spirit is baptizing His Church in fire by eradicating every word, deed and attitude out of our lives which does not glorify the Father. If we allow God to purge us, we will be made a vessel of honor.

"But who can endure the day of His coming? And who can stand when He appears? For He is like a refiner's fire and like launderers' soap. He will sit as a refiner and a purifier of silver; He will purify the sons of Levi, and purge them as gold and silver, that they may offer to the Lord an offering in righteousness." Malachi 3:2-3.

B. ILLUSTRATION FROM THE NATURAL REAL

Corn versus Johnson grass - Matthew 13:18-33

Johnson grass is every farmer's nightmare! **It is a <u>weed</u> which looks like corn when it grows next to it. It roots intertwine with good crops, <u>steals</u> their nutrients, and causes an <u>inferior</u> crop**.

1) Natural Progression:

From Seed ....

To Plant ....

To Mature Plant with Extensive Root System

2) Good seeds and bad seeds look alike when in seed form. Only extensive education and experience allows a farmer to recognize a seed for what it truly is. The same is true with the attitudes of our hearts.

3) A **bad** attitude left to itself will eventually sprout into a dangerous **weed** of wrong behavior.

4) Corn versus Johnson grass - **Johnson grass is a weed which typifies the development of a root problem in the spiritual realm.**

CHARACTERISTICS OF JOHNSON GRASS

- ⇨ It has an extensive root system which has joints every one to six inches.
- ⇨ Its roots are myriad and run in every direction.
- ⇨ It intertwines with the good roots of the corn plant.
- ⇨ When it grows with corn, it grows alongside and looks identical to corn.
- ⇨ When knee high, it cannot be pulled up without uprooting and destroying the good corn.
- ⇨ Johnson grass can be cut off at the ground level, but will immediately send up new shoots from the old shoots and from the underground joints. Hence - You cannot destroy the roots by simply cutting off the plant.
- ⇨ Johnson grass will continue to steal nutrients from the soil that should go to the cornstalk, thereby producing an inferior ear of corn.
- ⇨ Johnson grass cannot be destroyed in the growing season. Spraying it would kill the corn. It must be killed after the harvest, during the winter.
- ⇨ Johnson grass is killed by a deep plowing after harvest, raking the roots together and
    1. burning them,
    2. poisoning them, or
    3. leaving them to be killed by a hard winter freeze.

5) Spiritual Comparison: Many times, God will not deal with a spiritual problem during a productive ministry season. He will bring the individual into a "winter season" of inactivity and productivity (Recommended Reading - The Spiritual Seasons of Life by Evelyn Hamon). He will plow you upside down, exposing your problem and then:

    a) Spray them with a strong anointing to destroy or....
    b) Rake the individual's soul until all the roots are removed and thrown into the fire of God's purging.

C. EXAMPLES OF ROOT PROBLEMS

1. Root of Bitterness - Hebrews 12:15
2. Love of Money - Root of all evil - 1 Timothy 6:10

D. THESE PRINCIPLES APPLY TO EVERYONE

1) If you have a **wrong attitude** or a **bad habit** that you've repeated over **three** times, you probably have allowed it to go beyond the **seed stage** and has now sprouted roots.

2) We must deal with the situation before root problems become intertwined into your personality and performance.

3) Study to show yourself approved - in **word**, **deed**, and **attitude**. Your character is the foundation of your eternal ministry with Him.

4) Realize that every word, deed and attitude starts with the **thoughts** you choose to think.

   "I beseech you therefore, brethren, by the mercies of God, that you present your bodies a living sacrifice, holy, acceptable to God, which is your reasonable service. And do not be conformed to this world, but be transformed by the renewing of your mind, that you may prove what is that good and acceptable and perfect will of God." Romans 12:1-2.

   "For though we walk in the flesh, we do not war according to the flesh. For the weapons of our warfare are not carnal but mighty in God for pulling down strongholds, casting down arguments and every high thing that exalts itself against the knowledge of God, bringing every thought into captivity to the obedience of Christ, and being ready to punish all disobedience when your obedience is fulfilled." 2 Corinthians 10:3-6.

5) Be quick to repent!! When you see a weed seed, allow God to pull it out. If not, God will remove us from ministry in His Body just as sheep are separated from goats, good fish from bad fish, and tares from wheat. Matthew 25:32, 33; 13:29, 30, 47, 48

- **STUDENTS:** You will be lead in a prayer of repentance. Open your heart to the Holy Spirit and write down those areas which He has revealed as weed seeds. Extend your faith for the grace to overcome.

____

____

____

ADDITIONAL NOTES:

EZEKIEL & JEREMIAH'S PROBLEM WITH PERSECUTION

James 5:10

"My brethren, take the prophets, who spoke in the name of the Lord, as an example of suffering and patience."

I. EZEKIEL & JEREMIAH PROBABLY SUFFERED MORE SEVERE PERSONAL PERSECUTION THAN ANY OTHER OLD TESTAMENT PROPHETS.

A. EZEKIEL'S MINISTRY CHARACTERIZED BY PERSECUTION

"And you, son of man, do not be afraid of them nor be afraid of their words, though briers and thorns are with you and you dwell among scorpions; do not be afraid of their words or dismayed by their looks, though they are a rebellious house."

Ezekiel 2:6

B. JEREMIAH'S MINISTRY WAS ALSO CHARACTERIZED AND REWARDED BY PERSECUTION

"Now Pashhur the son of Immer, the priest who was also chief governor in the house of the Lord, heard that Jeremiah prophesied these things. Then Pashhur struck Jeremiah the prophet, and put him in the stocks that were in the high gate of Benjamin, which was by the house of the Lord."

Jeremiah 20:1-2

"Therefore the princes were angry with Jeremiah, and they struck him and put him in prison in the house of Jonathan the scribe. For they had made that the prison."

Jeremiah 37:15

"So they took Jeremiah and cast him into the dungeon of Malchiah the king's son, which was in the court of the prison, and they let Jeremiah down with ropes. And in the dungeon there was no water, but mire. So Jeremiah sank in the mire."

Jeremiah 38:6

II. SUFFERING IS THE STANDARD FOR THE PROPHETIC LIFE

When most people think of the prophets, they immediately think of great revelation, dynamic preaching, flowing prophecy, strong word of knowledge and word of wisdom and crowds of people being amazed who are falling down under the power of their greatness! ... BUT... James 5:10 states:

"My brethren, take the prophets, who spoke in the name of the Lord, as an example of suffering and patience."

Those who desire to speak for God must remember that the principal players in history - God, humanity and the devil - are still at work today. Therefore...

1. God still speaks through His people.
2. The devil does all he can to destroy the voice of God.
3. People still resent and resist God's prophetic word.

A. THERE IS NO PERFECTION WITHOUT SUFFERING!

1) Jesus is our example.
2) People, Pressure and Problems: suffering = patience
3) Tribulation brings about patience:

"And not only that, but we also glory in tribulations, knowing that tribulation produces perseverance."

Romans 5:3

B. YOU MUST SUFFER IN THE FLESH IN ORDER TO CEASE FROM SIN.

"Therefore, since Christ suffered for us in the flesh, arm yourselves also with the same mind, for he who has suffered in the flesh has ceased from sin."

1 Peter 4:1

C. THE SUCCESS IS IN THE ATTITUDE-SELF DENIAL IS THE SECRET!

"Then Jesus said to His disciples, "If anyone desires to come after Me, let him deny himself, and take up his cross, and follow Me.

Matthew 16:24

Prophetic people must take up their ministry crosses joyfully, denying themselves all the fleshly indulgences of these prophetic pitfalls, weed seed attitudes and syndromes.

D. Why do most Christians think trials are strange?

1) Don't think it strange concerning trials

"Beloved, do not think it strange concerning the fiery trial which is to try you, as though some strange thing happened to you; but rejoice to the extent that you partake of Christ's sufferings, that when His glory is revealed, you may also be glad with exceeding joy. If you are reproached for the name of Christ, blessed are you, for the Spirit of glory and of God rests upon you. On their part He is blasphemed, but on your part He is glorified."

1 Peter 4:12-14

2) The Amplified version states verse 12 as:

"Think it not strange concerning the fiery trails which come to test your quality of manhood as though something strange and unusual to you and your position were befalling you."

1 Peter 4:12, AMP

3) Persecution isn't strange, it's **standard**!

Remember that "all that live Godly in Christ Jesus," will suffer persecution.

4) If you are suffering for Christ's sake, REJOICE!

III. PROPHETIC PEOPLE SUFFER MORE PERSECUTION

A. "PAULINE PRINCIPLE"

1) **The more revelation, the more thorns of human persecution and demonic opposition.**

"And lest I should be exalted above measure by the abundance of the revelations, a thorn in the flesh was given to me, a messenger of Satan to buffet me, lest I be exalted above measure."

2 Corinthians 12:7

2) 2 Corinthians 12:1-7 - Paul didn't boast in his apostleship or his miracles, but he boasted in his weakness. An angel of Satan was sent to buffet Paul because of the abundance of revelation. Paul developed the proper biblical attitude as he states in verse 12:

"Truly the signs of an apostle were accomplished among you with all perseverance, in signs and wonders and mighty deeds."

2 Corinthians 12:12

3) Note that Paul's revelatory ministry was confirmed with not only signs, wonders and mighty deeds, but also with patience. The word patience in the original Greek text is the word υπομονή - hupomone - which means **to endure with a cheerful attitude**.

B. PROPHETS & APOSTLES RECEIVE THE MOST REVELATION

"Surely the Lord God does nothing, unless He reveals His secret to His servants the prophets."

Amos 3:7

"... which in other ages was not made known to the sons of men, as it has now been revealed by the Spirit to His holy apostles and prophets."

Ephesians 3:5

Both the apostle and prophet are revelation gift ministries.

C. JESUS IS SENDING APOSTLES AND PROPHETS; SOME WILL BE PERSECUTED AND KILLED

"Therefore the wisdom of God also said, 'I will send them prophets and apostles, and some of them they will kill and persecute,' that the blood of all the prophets which was shed from the foundation of the world may be required of this generation."

Luke 11:49-50

Note that it is the wisdom of God that sends the apostles and prophets. They will try to persecute and kill (not just physical but in reputation, influence, effectiveness, disallowance of anointing) the apostolic and prophetic ministry. Those called to this ministry gift cannot develop a persecution complex! Romans 8:28 must be remembered:

"And we know that all things work together for good to those who love God, to those who are the called according to His purpose."

Romans 8:28

We not only have to know that all things are working for our good, we must believe it!!

IV. WE MUST HAVE GRACE TO ADJUST

- We have no option but to adjust to persecution. If you cannot take persecution, rejection, and pressures from your peers, then you cannot survive as an end-time warrior in His army.
- Realize that grace is a companion with God's calling on your life. You can appropriate it by faith and obedience.
- The truth sets you free (John 8:32) and freedom causes you to rejoice!

"For all things are for your sakes, that grace, having spread through the many, may cause thanksgiving to abound to the glory of God. Therefore we do not lose heart. Even though our outward man is perishing, yet the inward man is being renewed day by day. For our light affliction, which is but for a moment, is working for us a far more exceeding and eternal weight of glory."

2 Corinthians 4:15-17

- Not one scripture in the Bible gives us the right to **moan** and **complain**. The word of God says **REJOICE** in all things.

➢ STUDENT: Ask the Lord to help you make attitude adjustments.

ADDITIONAL NOTES:

JOSEPH'S DIVINE OPTIMISM
VS.
JACOB'S HUMAN PESSIMISM

> Romans 8:28
> *"And we know that all things work together for good to those who love God, to those who are the called according to His purpose"*

The biblical characters of Joseph and Jacob provide us with a useful study in contrast with regard to their attitudes toward life and ministry.

Read Genesis 47:9; 42:36; 45:5-8; 50:20; Romans 8:28, 31, 32, 37; 2 Corinthians 4:15-17

I. JACOB'S PESSIMISM

Jacob is typical of the present-day prophet with a **persecution complex** and a **negative attitude** toward people and the ministry. (See Genesis 42:36; 47:9)

A. A LIFE OF CONFLICT

1. Jacob had to leave home because of conflict with his father and older brothers. (This is typical of the prophetic minister who has had to leave his or her denomination or home church over conflict with denominational leaders or a local pastor.)

2. Jacob worked under his uncle Laban, a man who constantly tried to use him, deceive him, and manipulate him into building his own kingdom. Jacob eventually had to outwit and manipulate Laban in order to survive and prosper.

B. "ALL THINGS ARE AGAINST ME"

1. See Genesis 42:36 and Genesis 47:9

2. When Jacob met God and was transformed, he ceased his manipulating methods, but he retained a negative attitude. Every time something unpleasant happened to him he concluded, *"All things are against me"* Genesis 47:9

C. THOSE WITH JACOB'S "WEED SEED ATTITUDE" NEED INNER HEALING & SUPERNATURAL TRANSFORMATION

Those with Jacob's background and personality will have to work continually to overcome the feeling that others are trying to use them. Without counsel and healing, every tragedy or setback will bring a response of **pessimism, discouragement, self-pity and complaining, with periods of non-productivity**.

II. JOSEPH'S PERSPECTIVE & SELFLESS SPIRIT

A. HAVING GOD'S ETERNAL PURPOSE

Because Joseph had God's eternal purpose within his view, he was allowed to see from God's perspective and he never lost faith about God's original communication in his dreams.

B. PROVIDENCE OF GOD

1. The word "providence" means **divine guidance or care**.
2. Joseph believed that everything that happened to him was **providentially ordained by God**. He declared to his brothers:

   "Not you, but God sent me to Egypt; you meant all that you did to me for evil, but God meant it to me for good." Genesis 45:5-8; 50:20

C. APOSTLE PAUL - NEW TESTAMENT COUNTERPART

1. Apostle Paul had the same perspective as Joseph. Paul declared in Romans 8:28:

   "And we know that all things work together for good to those who love God, to those who are the called according to His purpose."

2) Those with Joseph's and Paul's perspective on life will:

   a) believe that God is providentially directing the affairs of their lives as they seek to do His will and fulfill His purpose;
   b) **quickly forgive, and even bless, those who have used or abused them , as they repent.**

III. IMPORTANCE OF PROPER ATTITUDE

It is not what we go through in life, but our spirit and attitude that determine the outcome of our life and ministry. How should we react?

- Be thankful! - Ephesians 5:20
- Be forgiving! - Ephesians 4:32
- Rejoice! - 1 Thessalonians 5:16
- Be positive! - Philippians 4:8
- Be victorious! - 1 John 5:4
- Proper attitude is based upon: Romans 8:28; 1 Corinthians 4:15; 1 Thessalonians 5:16-18

IV. BE OPEN TO CORRECTION

A foolish prophet or prophetic person will **resent** and **resist correction**, instruction and adjustment. A wise person will respond according to Proverbs 1:5; 9:8-9 (AMP):

"The wise will hear and increase in learning, and the person of understanding will acquire skill and attain to godly counsel so that he may be able to steer his course rightly .... Reprove not a scorner, lest he hate you; reprove a wise man, and he will love you. Give instruction to a wise man and he will be yet wiser; tea.ch a righteous man [one upright and in right standing with God] and he will increase with learning."

A. IN THE EYES OF A SCORNER, CORRECTION MEANS REJECTION

When trying to correct someone with a spirit of rejection, they will feel you are against them and out to hinder or destroy them. So even correction given in love with great tactfulness by delegated authority is almost impossible for them to hear, receive and act upon in the spirit of wisdom.

B. PRAYERFULLY CONSIDER ALL COUNSEL GIVEN

When receiving any suggestion concerning the need for adjustment, prayerfully consider it before disregarding it. It could be the piece of counsel that saves you from the devil's pitfall and ultimate destruction of your life and ministry.

➢ **STUDENT:** Thank God in all things, even what seemed to be harmful and hurt their feelings. Make a commitment to develop the optimism of Joseph and the positive faith and attitude of the Apostle Paul.

ADDITIONAL NOTES:

ACTIVATIONS

To activate is to stir up the gifts of the spirit within, or make them become active. We are exhorted in 1 Peter 4:10, "*As each one has received a gift, minister it to one another, as good stewards of the manifold grace of God.*"

The activation portion of this module gives saints a *safe place* to exercise their faith in manifesting spiritual gifts. Because it is just practice, they have an opportunity to overcome any fears in moving in spiritual gifts.

BRIEF OVERVIEW OF ACTIVATIONS

I. EXPLANATION OF ACTIVATIONS

What does "activation" mean? Why do we activate? How does it work?

A. Definition

We are going to set up a situation where we will ask you to hear from God, and then communicate what you get from God, under these conditions:

1. Do it the way we ask you to do it.
2. Give permission for others in the room to make a mistake, including yourself.

EXHORTATION:

Students, remember that fear brings a snare. It controls you by keeping you from doing what you are supposed to do. Fear is anti-faith. Fear kills faith because you don't act. Faith is doing something. Activating is acting. Step past your fears. Remember, God has given you a **spirit of power, love, and a sound mind!**

B. Why do we activate?

1. Sports analogy: When you want to be excellent in sports, you train. While you train, you may do things that have nothing to do with the actual sport you are training for. For example, swimmers do weight training; boxers run in training; runners do sit-ups. These types of things develop strength, flexibility, and endurance. When athletes are actually in competition, the activities they performed in training will be put to use. It's the same with activations. We are training you to hear God's voice in a safe atmosphere, so that when the "real life" situations arise, you will have more confidence and ability.

2. When we are doing activations, we are in the gym, speaking metaphorically. We will ask you to do things. When you are in training, there are no mistakes. The only way you can fail in training is by not training! You will find your limits and break through them. For example, you may be asked to prophesy to someone you don't know, someone you can't see, for a short time, for a long time, behind someone, or in front of someone.

C. Rules

1. Don't take a word you receive in training and treat it the same as you would in the competition. Go for it and mess up! Mistakes are okay. No one is perfect when they start.
2. The gifts are developed by reason of use. Press through barriers.
3. We are stewards of the gifts He has given. Don't bury your gift.

Take a risk.

II. KEY POINTS/FEEDBACK

After receiving feedback from students after the activation, they may have related to some of the following key points:

- ⇨ You heard a phrase, or saw a picture. It's like a Polaroid camera. Let God develop it. Don't make it develop or try to interpret it yourself.
- ⇨ It's okay if what you received was not specific. It may seem vague to them, but very specific to person receiving the word.
- ⇨ It may not make sense to them you but perfect sense to person receiving the word.
- ⇨ God knows what the receiver needs. If you get something very general, like "God loves you" or "He is well pleased with you". It may be a rhema to the receiver, and exactly what they needed at that time.
- ⇨ Person may not relate to the word at that time. It may have been something in the past that they had forgotten about, or something they may relate to in the future.
- ⇨ Person may relate to some of the word, but not all of it. Don't throw the baby out with the bath water. Put what you don't understand on the shelf.

III. ACTIVATION GUIDELINES

1. There is a special time and place to be activated. Don't do it elsewhere without proper oversight.

2. Don't make any major decisions on a prophetic word you receive in an activation time. Allow God to confirm it independently by established ministers and wise counsel.

3. Write out your word as soon as possible. Keep it in a notebook with the rest of your prophecies.

4. Counsel with your pastor/elder about all words you receive.

5. Seek to edify the Body when ministering spiritual gifts.

6. Be teachable.

7. Flow with the order of the service.

8. Give personal words only under pastoral supervision.